MW01630347

The recycling themed, *Where In The World Is Away*, is musician
**Michael Franti's** second children's book (*What I Be*, 2006).
Journey with Little Lee and Little Lou as they attempt to find a
place to throw their juice bottle "Away" only to encounter Mo
the Crow, who helps them discover that "AWAY," is really just
"SOMEWHERE ELSE" and flies them through the wondrous world
of recycling.

Known for his versatile illustration style of over twenty books,
the award-winning Canadian based **Ben Hodson** magically
illustrates his second collaboration (*What I Be*, 2006)
with Michael Franti. *Where In The World Is Away's* hilarious
rhyming tale also comes with a raucous read along CD
featuring Franti's hysterical family and friends. This book will
have you and your children laughing and smiling, all while learn-
ing about the importance of preserving our amazing planet!

www.MichaelFranti.com
www.BenHodson.ca

# Hey Everyone...

## "Where in the World is Away"...

- ✔ is printed and manufactured in the USA!

- ✔ is printed with environmentally-friendly soy ink!

- ✔ is printed on elemental chlorine-free (ECF), sustainably harvested, recycled stock!

This book is dedicated to My sons Adé and Cappy,
and to my mother Carole, who adopted me and taught me,
and hundreds of other children around the world the joy of reading.
~ Michael Franti


To my daughters, Zoe and Alex and to all the kids
who are trying to make this world a better place.
~ Ben Hodson

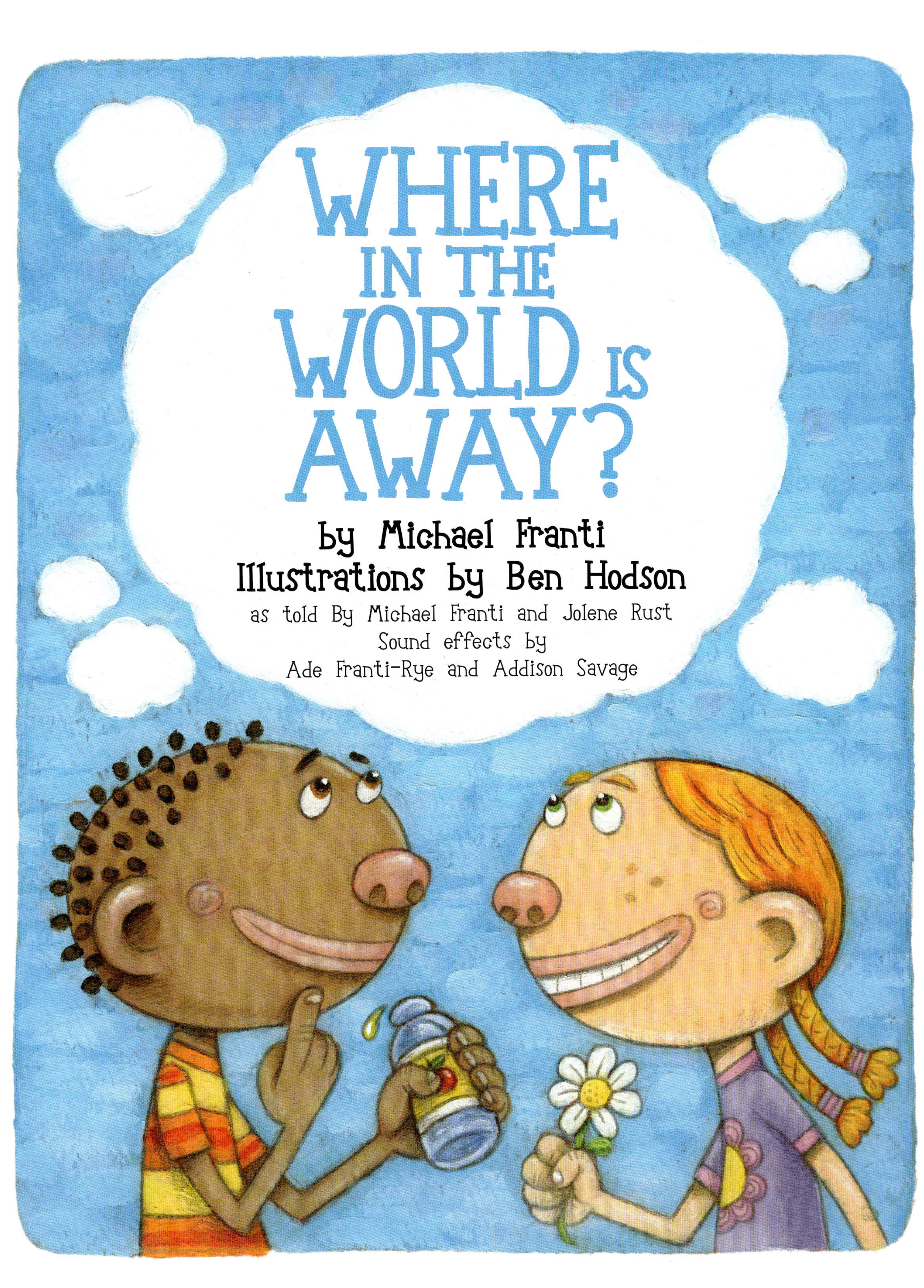

WHERE IN THE WORLD IS AWAY?
by Michael Franti
Illustrations by Ben Hodson
as told By Michael Franti and Jolene Rust
Sound effects by
Ade Franti-Rye and Addison Savage

PARK

Little Lee and Little Lou
sat by a lake sharing a bottle of juice.

It was a warm, sunny day and the birds
were at play,
and they smiled as they watched Mama Goose.

As they finished the drink,
Lou pulled back his arm
and said, "I'm gonna throw
it AWAY."

"Stop Lou, think! Before we make a mistake!
Where in the world is AWAY?

If we throw it in the lake
it's gone for today, but is that really AWAY?"

"Not for the frogs
who hip hop on the logs

or the fish who
jump up in the air.

Or the little tiny things
that live off the greens

that grow
on the bottom
down there."

"All of our spills just fill up their gills
and it's so hard to breathe without air.
MOTOR OIL
BATTERY

They play hide and go seek,
and think school is cool
so we shouldn't
make a mess down there."

"I've got a plan," Lou started to say, "Over the hill's where I'll throw it AWAY!"

"Not so fast Lou, if I may say, is over the hill there, really AWAY?"

"That's where the forest grows
tall and wide
and all kinds of critters live deep inside.

It's cool in the daytime and warm at night
and squirrels do twirls
while birds are in flight."

"There's nuts and there's berries,
there's bears and there's fairies
and a butterfly up in a tree.
By the light of the moon,
they play drums with raccoons
as the mice shout,
"one-two-threeeeeee!!!"

But if the forest has bottles
on a hot sunny day
the sun magnifies and
might set it ablaze.
Then all the forest beings
would run with a fright.
"We don't want that Lou!"
"NO, YOU'RE RIGHT!"

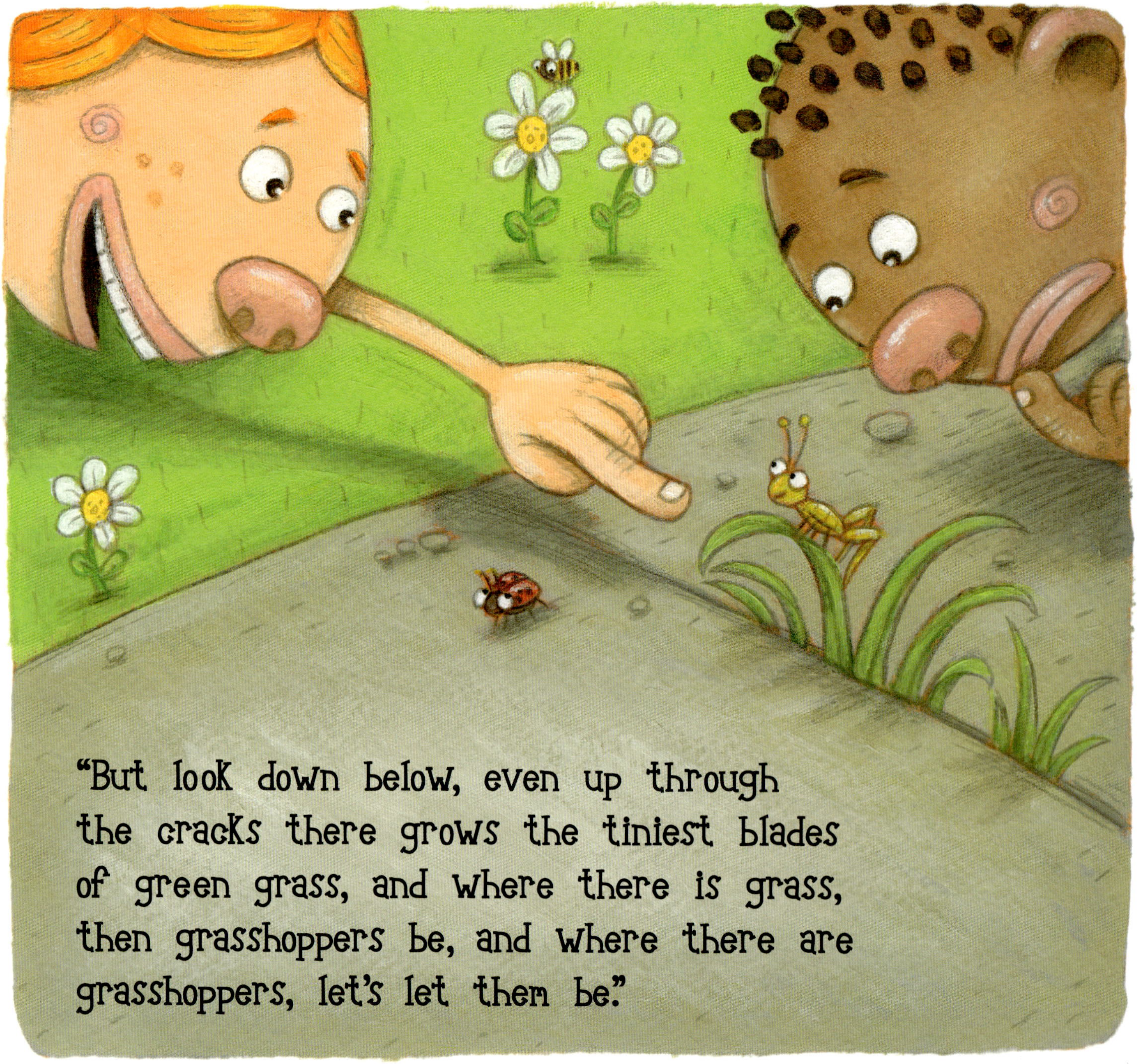

"But look down below, even up through
the cracks there grows the tiniest blades
of green grass, and where there is grass,
then grasshoppers be, and where there are
grasshoppers, let's let them be."

"And besides, we all like
to keep the street neat
and we don't need glass where
there might be bare feet.

There's far too much garbage
it's just got to stop
the landfills are filling
right up to the top."

"Then where is AWAY?"
said confused Little Lou,

"And what of the bottle
when there's no more juice?"

They spotted a bin with a round symbol on it,
a can with the word "RECYCLING" on it,
and inside the can there were hundreds of bottles
in all kinds of shapes and colors and models.

"If we put it in there,
will it go AWAY?"
Sweet Little Lou started to say.

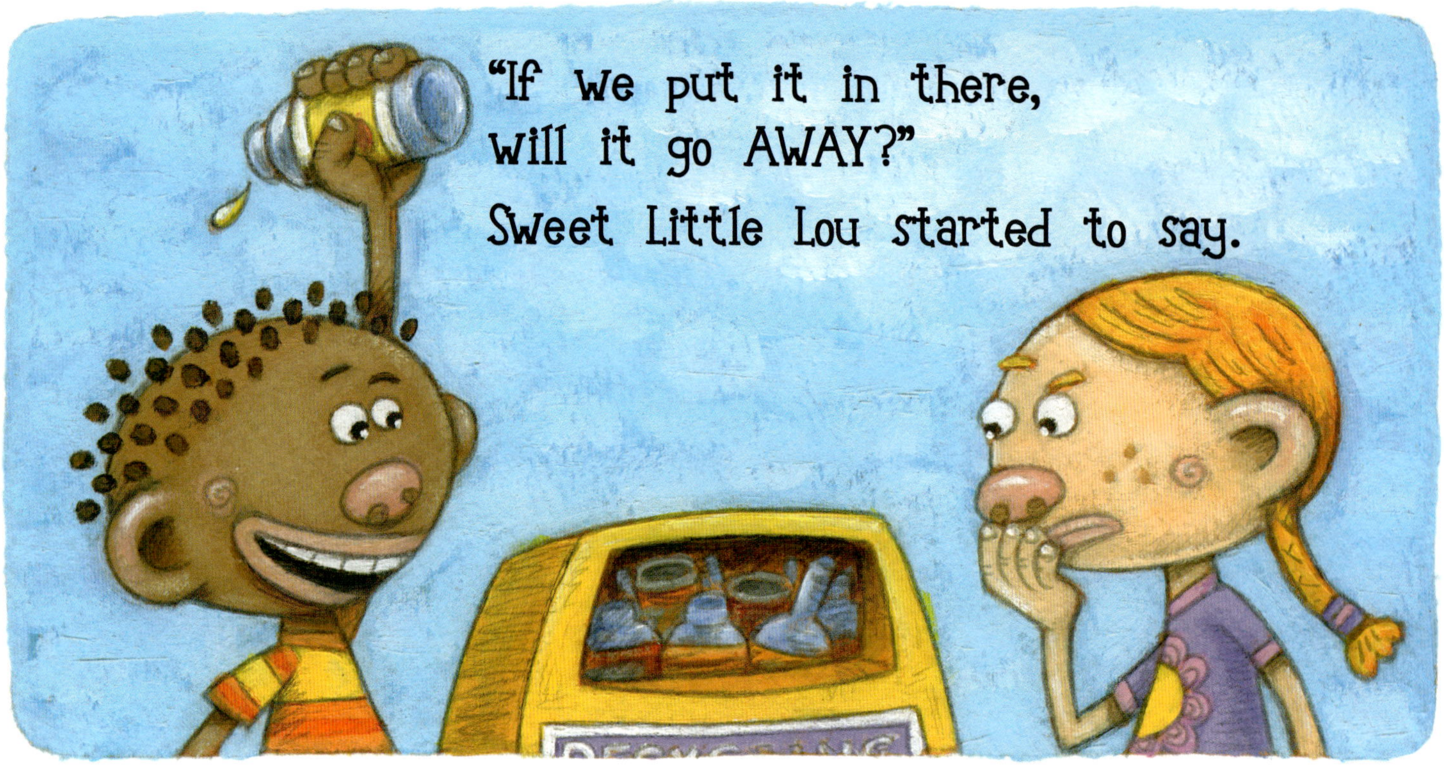

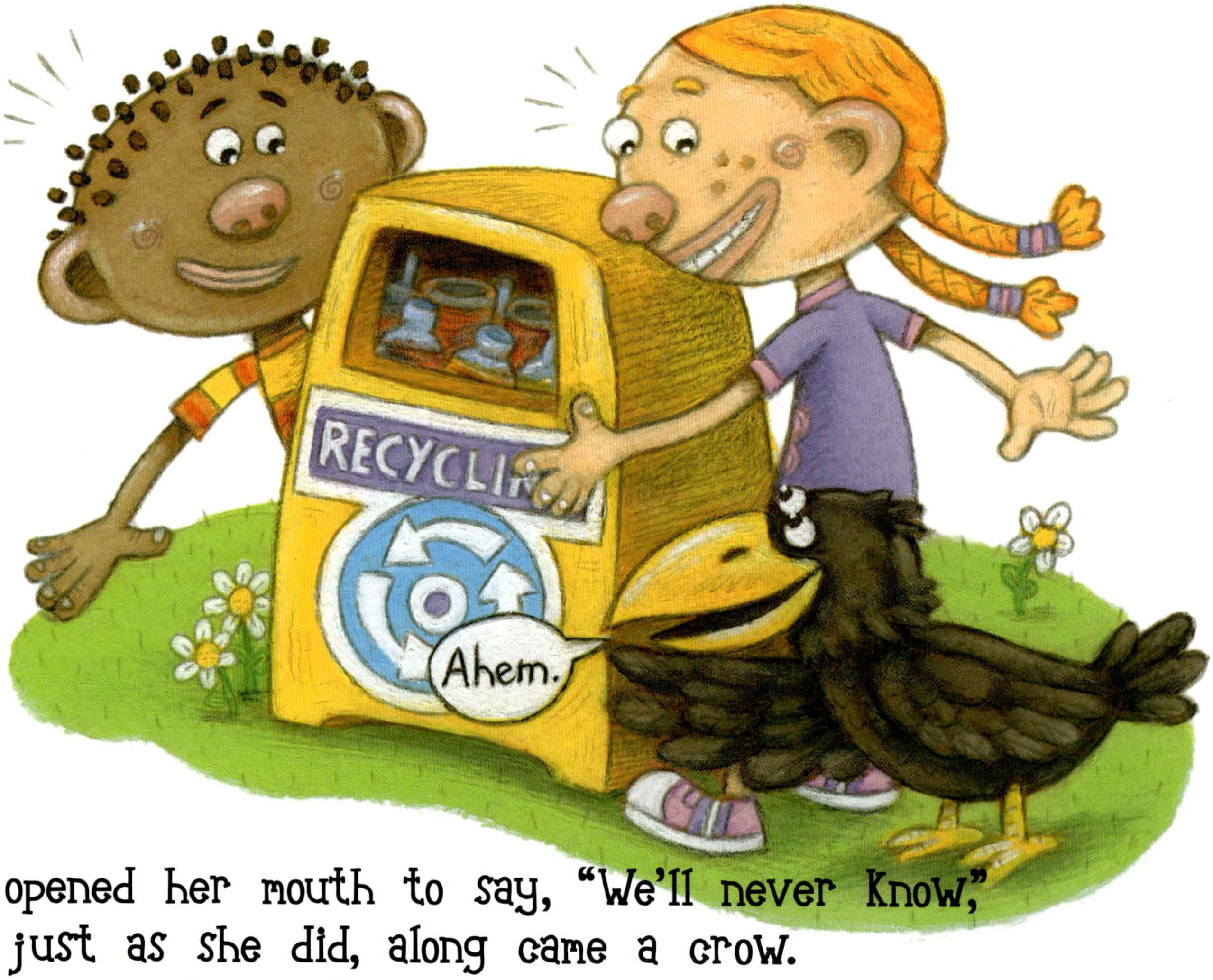


Lee opened her mouth to say, "We'll never know,"
and just as she did, along came a crow.
This crow at her feet, was oh so unique,
a crow named Mo with a beak that could speak!

"Good heavens!" They shouted, "How could this be?"
The crow said, "Relax, it's just little old me.
If you'd like to know where old bottles should go,
close your eyes, spread your wings
and follow this crow!"

"The bottles are picked up by truck and transported to a glass sorting center, where then they are sorted.

Green ones go there and brown ones go here,
there's places for blue and for yellow and clear."
RECYCLING DEPOT

"All of the paper and caps are removed
and, yes, even those things
are RECYCLED too."

"All of the glass gets crushed
into 'cullet,' a word you mightn't heard,
but that's what they call it."

"Then it's thrown into a furnace to heat
to a temperature of over two thousand degrees!!!
And then when it's melted, it glows into goo,
and then there are so many things you can do."

"You can bend it and shape it
and pour it into moulds,
make magical artwork,
or things to be sold.

And when it cools down
it turns hard very fast
and quickly returns
into shiny smooth glass."

"It makes mirrors and lamps
and grape jelly jars,
even eyeglasses and windows for cars.

There's so many things, so many to choose
and, yes, you can even make bottles for juice."

"So always RECYCLE," said crow with a smile
"and REDUCE what you use every once in a while.
When you reach for that bottle high up on the shelf,
remember 'AWAY' is just SOMEWHERE ELSE."

"There's so many choices," said sweet Little Lou…
"But this here bottle we're going to RE-USE…"

…and they each put a flower in it.

The End

# Tell your own story.

## How can you reduce?

_______________________________________

_______________________________________

_______________________________________

## How can you reuse?

_______________________________________

_______________________________________

_______________________________________

## How can you recycle?

_______________________________________

_______________________________________

_______________________________________

Published by
Stay Human Books
2180 Bryant St. Ste. 206, San Francisco, CA 94110
www.WhereInTheWorldIsAway.com

ISBN 978-0-578-10086-9
Library of Congress Control Number: 2012931815

The artwork in this book was created using acrylic paint and colored pencil on watercolor paper.
-Ben Hodson

Original Type Design by Carla Swanson
Produced/Printed by Dante Orazzi, CreativeBeans.com
CD Sound Engineering by J Bowman

Printed in the U.S.A. on Elemental Chlorine-Free (ECF), Sustainably Harvested/Recycled Stock
with Environmentally Friendly Soy Ink